SACRAMENTO PUBLIC LIBRARY
828 "I" Street
Sacramento, CA 95814
05/17

EASY GENIUS MATH

DECIMALS AND FRACTIONS

IT'S EASY!

Rebecca Wingard-Nelson

Enslow Publishers, Inc.
40 Industrial Road
Box 398
Berkeley Heights, NJ 07922
USA

http://www.enslow.com

Original edition published as *Decimals and Fractions* in 2008.

Library of Congress Cataloging-in-Publication Data

Wingard-Nelson, Rebecca.
    Decimals and fractions: it's easy / Rebecca Wingard-Nelson.
        p. cm. — (Easy genius math)
    Originally published: Berkeley Heights, NJ: Enslow Publishers, c2008.
    Summary: "Learn how to add and subtract like and unlike fractions. Write fractions
    and decimals as percents, and learn how to estimate"—Provided by publisher.
    Includes bibliographical references and index.
    ISBN 978-0-7660-4252-0
    1. Decimal fractions—Juvenile literature. 2. Fractions—Juvenile literature. I. Title.
    QA117.W556 2014
    513.2'6—dc23

                                                                            2012042853

Future editions:
Paperback ISBN: 978-1-4644-0447-4   EPUB ISBN: 978-1-4645-1243-8
Single-User PDF ISBN: 978-1-4646-1243-5   Multi-User PDF ISBN: 978-0-7660-5875-0

Printed in the United States of America

102013 Lake Book Manufacturing, Inc., Melrose Park, IL

10 9 8 7 6 5 4 3 2 1

To Our Readers: We have done our best to make sure all Internet addresses in this book were active and appropriate when we went to press. However, the author and the publisher have no control over and assume no liability for the material available on those Internet sites or on other Web sites they may link to. Any comments or suggestions can be sent by e-mail to comments@enslow.com or to the address on the back cover.

♻ Enslow Publishers, Inc., is committed to printing our books on recycled paper. The paper in every book contains 10% to 30% post-consumer waste (PCW). The cover board on the outside of each book contains 100% PCW. Our goal is to do our part to help young people and the environment too!

Illustration Credits: Artisticco LLC/Photos.com, p. 23; © Clipart.com, pp. 9, 14, 38, 46, 54; iStockphoto/Thinkstock, pp. 33, 36, 44; Jupiterimages/Photos.com, p. 52; Nicolas Amelio Ortiz/Photos.com, p. 60; Shutterstock.com, pp. 12, 16, 21, 29, 41, 43, 48, 57.

Cover Photo: Shutterstock.com

CONTENTS

Introduction

Not every person is an accountant, engineer, rocket scientist, or math teacher. However, every person does use math.

Most people never think, "I just used math to decide if I have enough milk for this week!" But that is exactly what they did. Math is everywhere; we just don't see it because it doesn't always look like the math we do at school.

Math gives you the power to:
• determine the best route on a trip
• keep score in a game
• choose the better buy
• figure a sale price
• plan a vacation schedule

People use fractions every day to measure all sorts of things. You use fractions of a cup or teaspoon, fractions of an inch, and fractions of a pound. Decimals are used all over the world in sports and science. They are also used to represent money values.

This book will help you understand decimals and fractions. It can be read from beginning to end, or used to review a specific topic.

What numbers can you use to describe part of a group? What numbers can you use to describe part of one thing?

Fractions

Fractions use two numbers to describe part of a whole thing, or part of a group.

numerator—The top number in a fraction. It tells the number of parts being talked about. 1 part of the star is colored.

denominator—The bottom number in a fraction. It tells the total number of equal parts. The star has 2 equal parts.

$\frac{1}{2}$ **is colored.**

Part of a Group

Two men are standing at a bus stop. Only one has an umbrella. Use a fraction to describe how many of the men have umbrellas.

Step 1: How many men are in the whole group? 2. The number 2 is the bottom number, or denominator.

$$\frac{}{2}$$

Step 2: How many men have umbrellas? 1. The number 1 is the top number, or numerator.

$$\frac{1}{2}$$

$\frac{1}{2}$ **of the men have umbrellas.**

proper fraction—A fraction whose numerator is less than its denominator.	$\dfrac{5}{8}$
	$5 < 8$
improper fraction—A fraction whose numerator is equal to or greater than its denominator.	$\dfrac{4}{3}$
	$4 > 3$

Part of a Whole

Use a fraction to tell how much of the rectangle is colored.

Step 1: How many equal parts are in the rectangle? 8.
The denominator is 8.

$$\dfrac{}{8}$$

Step 2: How many of the equal parts are colored? 5.
The numerator is 5.

$$\dfrac{5}{8}$$

$\dfrac{5}{8}$ of the rectangle is colored.

The **fraction bar**
is the line that separates the
numerator and denominator.

$\dfrac{5}{8}$ ⟵ fraction bar

Sometimes fractions are written with
a slash in place of the fraction bar.

5/8

↑
numerator slash denominator

7

Can you write a fraction with a value of one or more? Yes! You can use an improper fraction or a mixed fraction.

whole number

mixed fraction—A number that is made of two parts: a whole number and a proper fraction. $2\frac{3}{5}$ ← fraction

Mixed Fractions and Improper Fractions

Write a mixed fraction and an improper fraction to show how many circles are colored.

Step 1: How many full circles are colored? 1. This is the whole number part.

$1-$

Step 2: How many equal parts are in the partially colored circle? 4. This is the denominator of the fraction part.

$1\frac{}{4}$

Step 3: How many equal parts of the partially colored circle are colored? 1. This is the numerator of the fraction part.

$1\frac{1}{4}$
mixed fraction

Step 4: The denominator of an improper fraction is how many equal parts are in one whole. How many equal parts are in one whole circle? 4. This is the denominator.

$\frac{}{4}$

Step 5: How many equal parts are colored in all of the circles (whole and partially colored)? 5. This is the numerator.

$\frac{5}{4}$
improper fraction

$1\frac{1}{4}$, or $\frac{5}{4}$, circles are colored. $1\frac{1}{4}$ and $\frac{5}{4}$ are equal in value.

Renaming Improper Fractions

Write $\frac{7}{4}$ as a mixed fraction.

Step 1: Divide the numerator by the denominator.

$$\begin{array}{r} 1\text{R}3 \\ 4\overline{)7} \\ -4 \\ \hline 3 \end{array}$$

Step 2: Write the mixed fraction.
The remainder is the numerator of the fraction part.
The denominator stays the same.

$1\frac{3}{4}$

$\frac{7}{4} = 1\frac{3}{4}$

Renaming Mixed Fractions

Ami used $3\frac{1}{2}$ cups of apples for a pie. Write the amount of apples as an improper fraction.

Step 1: Find the new numerator.
Multiply the whole number by the denominator, then add the numerator.

$$3\frac{1}{2} = \frac{(3 \times 2) + 1}{2} = \frac{7}{2}$$

Step 2: Keep the same denominator.

$$\frac{7}{2}$$

Ami used $\frac{7}{2}$ cups of apples.

③ Equivalent Fractions

If your name were Jacob Robert, people could call you Jacob, Jake, Jay, or JR. Fractions also have different names that mean the same thing.

Equivalent Fractions

Find another name for the fraction $\frac{1}{2}$.

Step 1: Fold a strip of paper into two equal pieces. Color one of the pieces to show $\frac{1}{2}$.

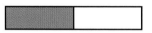

Step 2: Fold each half of the strip into two equal pieces. The strip now has four equal sections.

Step 3: Write a fraction using the four equal sections as the denominator.

$\frac{2 \text{ colored sections}}{4 \text{ total sections}}$

$\frac{2}{4}$ is the same as $\frac{1}{2}$.

> **Equivalent** means equal in value.
> $\frac{1}{2}$ and $\frac{2}{4}$ are equivalent fractions.

Multiply

Find a fraction that is equivalent to $\frac{2}{3}$.

Step 1: Multiply the numerator and denominator by the same number to find equivalent fractions. This is the same as multiplying by 1. (See page 17.)

Multiply the numerator and denominator by 2.

$$\frac{2}{3} = \frac{2 \times 2}{3 \times 2} = \frac{4}{6}$$

$\frac{2}{3} = \frac{4}{6}$ $\frac{2}{3}$ and $\frac{4}{6}$ are equivalent fractions.

Factors

Factors help you write equivalent fractions and reduce fractions to lowest terms.

factors—Numbers that divide evenly into a given number.

common factors—Numbers that divide evenly into a set of numbers. The number 2 divides evenly into 8 and 10. The number 2 is a common factor of 8 and 10.

greatest common factor—The largest number that divides evenly into a set of numbers.

Divide

Write the fraction $\frac{10}{40}$ in lowest terms.

Step 1: Find the greatest common factor of 10 and 40.

List the factors of 10:   **1, 2, 5, 10**

List the factors of 40:   **1, 2,** 4, **5,** 8, **10,** 20, 40

The common factors of 10 and 40 are 1, 2, 5, and 10.
The greatest common factor is 10.

Step 2: Write the fraction in lowest terms by dividing the numerator and denominator by their greatest common factor, 10. This is the same as dividing by 1.

$$\frac{10}{40} = \frac{10 \div 10}{40 \div 10} = \frac{1}{4}$$

$$\frac{10}{40} = \frac{1}{4}$$

A fraction is in **lowest terms** when the numerator and denominator do not have any common factors except 1.

Fractions in lowest terms are sometimes called fractions in **simplest form**.

④ Comparing Fractions

Which is greater, 2 or 3? Which is greater, $\frac{1}{2}$ or $\frac{2}{3}$? Fractions can be compared just like whole numbers.

Like and Unlike

like fractions—Fractions that have the same denominator (a *common* denominator). $\frac{1}{4}$ and $\frac{3}{4}$ are like fractions.

unlike fractions—Fractions that have different denominators. $\frac{1}{2}$ and $\frac{5}{6}$ are unlike fractions.

Comparing Like Fractions

Dee and Moira had the same number of math problems for homework. Dee finished $\frac{4}{5}$ of the problems. Moira finished $\frac{3}{5}$ of the problems. Who finished more of the problems?

To solve this problem, compare $\frac{4}{5}$ and $\frac{3}{5}$.

Step 1: To compare like fractions, only compare the numerators.

$4 > 3$, so $\frac{4}{5} > \frac{3}{5}$

Dee finished more of the problems than Moira.

Multiples

Multiples help you compare and order unlike fractions.
They will also help you add and subtract unlike fractions.

multiple—The product of a number and any whole number is a multiple of that number. Multiples of 3 are 3, 6, 9, . . .

common multiples—Numbers that are multiples of two or more numbers in a group.

least common multiple—The smallest multiple, other than zero, that two or more numbers have in common.

Comparing Unlike Fractions

Compare $\frac{1}{2}$ and $\frac{5}{8}$.

> The least common multiple of denominators is called the **least common denominator**.

Step 1: Write unlike fractions as like fractions using the least common denominator. Find the least common multiple of the denominators, 2 and 8.

List the multiples of 2:   2, 4, 6, **8**, 10, 12, . . .
List the multiples of 8:   **8**, 16, 24, 32, 40, . . .

The least common multiple of 2 and 8 is 8.

Step 2: Write both fractions with a denominator of 8.

To change a denominator of 2 to a denominator of 8, multiply the numerator and denominator by 4, because $2 \times 4 = 8$.

$$\frac{1}{2} = \frac{1 \times 4}{2 \times 4} = \frac{4}{8} \qquad \frac{5}{8} \text{ already has 8 as the denominator.}$$

Step 3: Compare like fractions by comparing the numerators.

$4 < 5$, so $\frac{4}{8} < \frac{5}{8}$

$\frac{1}{2} < \frac{5}{8}$

> Symbols are used to compare numbers
> < means   is less than
> > means   is greater than
> = means   is equal to

⑤ Adding Like Fractions

When fractions have the same denominator, addition is easy.

Adding Like Fractions

Mark ate $\frac{3}{8}$ of a deluxe pizza. Garth ate another $\frac{3}{8}$ of the pizza. What fraction of the pizza did they eat together? Write the answer in lowest terms.

To solve this problem, add.

$$\frac{3}{8} + \frac{3}{8}$$

Step 1: To add like fractions, add only the numerators.

$$\frac{3}{8} + \frac{3}{8} = \frac{3+3}{} = \frac{6}{}$$

Step 2: Keep the same denominator.

$$\frac{3}{8} + \frac{3}{8} = \frac{6}{8}$$

Step 3: Write the answer in lowest terms. Divide the numerator and denominator by their greatest common factor, 2.

$$\frac{6}{8} = \frac{6 \div 2}{8 \div 2} = \frac{3}{4}$$

$$\frac{3}{8} + \frac{3}{8} = \frac{3}{4}$$

Together, they ate $\frac{3}{4}$ **of the pizza.**

Adding Like Mixed Fractions

Add $3\frac{1}{3} + 2\frac{1}{3}$.

Step 1: Add the fractions.

$$\frac{1}{3} + \frac{1}{3} = \frac{1+1}{3} = \frac{2}{3}$$

Step 2: Add the whole numbers.

$$3 + 2 = 5$$

Step 3: Add the sum of the whole numbers and the sum of the fractions.

$$5 + \frac{2}{3} = 5\frac{2}{3}$$

$$3\frac{1}{3} + 2\frac{1}{3} = 5\frac{2}{3}$$

Regrouping names the same value in a different way.

Regrouping Mixed Fractions

Add $3\frac{3}{4} + 5\frac{2}{4}$.

Step 1: Add the fractions.

$$\frac{3}{4} + \frac{2}{4} = \frac{3+2}{4} = \frac{5}{4}$$

Step 2: Regroup the fraction sum. Write the improper fraction as a mixed number by dividing the numerator by the denominator. The quotient is the whole number part. The remainder is the new numerator.

$$4\overline{)5} \quad 1\text{R}1$$

$$\frac{5}{4} = 1\frac{1}{4}$$

Step 3: Add the whole numbers.

$$3 + 5 = 8$$

Step 4: Add the sum of the whole numbers and the sum of the fractions.

$$8 + 1\frac{1}{4} = 9\frac{1}{4}$$

$$3\frac{3}{4} + 5\frac{2}{4} = 9\frac{1}{4}$$

Fractions with different denominators need to be written as like fractions before they can be added.

Unlike Fractions

Phillip transferred $\frac{1}{2}$ of the music on his mp3 player from his own CDs. Another $\frac{1}{3}$ of the music came from his sister's CDs. What fraction of Phillip's mp3 music came from his and his sister's CDs?

To solve this problem, add. $\qquad \frac{1}{2} + \frac{1}{3}$

Step 1: Before you can add unlike fractions, you need to make the denominators the same. Find the least common multiple of the denominators, 2 and 3.

List the multiples of 2:   2, 4, **6**, 8, 10, 12, . . .
List the multiples of 3:   3, **6**, 9, 12, 15, . . .

The least common multiple of 2 and 3 is 6. Write both fractions with a denominator of 6.

$$\frac{1}{2} = \frac{1 \times 3}{2 \times 3} = \frac{3}{6} \qquad \frac{1}{3} = \frac{1 \times 2}{3 \times 2} = \frac{2}{6}$$

Step 2: Write the problem using like fractions.

$$\frac{1}{2} + \frac{1}{3}$$
is the same as $\frac{3}{6} + \frac{2}{6}$

Step 3: Add the numerators. Keep the common denominator.

$$\frac{3}{6} + \frac{2}{6} = \frac{3 + 2}{6} = \frac{5}{6}$$

$\frac{5}{6}$ of Phillip's mp3 music is from his and his sister's CDs.

Unlike Mixed Fractions

Add $6\frac{1}{4} + 8\frac{1}{2}$.

Step 1: Add the fractions.
Find a common denominator, then add.

$$\frac{1}{4} + \frac{1}{2}$$

$$\frac{1}{4} + \frac{2}{4}$$

$$\frac{1}{4} + \frac{2}{4} = \frac{1+2}{4} = \frac{3}{4}$$

Step 2: Add the whole numbers.

$$6 + 8 = 14$$

Step 3: Add the sum of the whole numbers and the sum of the fractions.

$$14 + \frac{3}{4} = 14\frac{3}{4}$$

$$6\frac{1}{4} + 8\frac{1}{2} = 14\frac{3}{4}$$

Why Can You Do That?

The Property of One says that when you multiply any number by 1, the value of the number does not change.

$$6 \times 1 = 6 \qquad 50 \times 1 = 50$$

When you multiply a numerator and denominator by the same number, you are really just multiplying the fraction by 1. The value of the fraction does not change.

$$\frac{1}{5} = \frac{1 \times 2}{5 \times 2} = \frac{2}{10} \qquad \frac{1}{4} = \frac{1 \times 3}{4 \times 3} = \frac{3}{12}$$

$$\frac{2}{2} = 1 \qquad\qquad \frac{3}{3} = 1$$

Subtracting
Like Fractions

(7)

Fractions are subtracted
the same way they are added.

Like Fractions

Subtract $\frac{3}{7} - \frac{1}{7}$.

Step 1: To subtract like fractions, subtract only the numerators. Keep the common denominator.

$$\frac{3}{7} - \frac{1}{7} = \frac{3-1}{7} = \frac{2}{7}$$

$$\frac{3}{7} - \frac{1}{7} = \frac{2}{7}$$

Subtracting From a Whole Number

Subtract $3 - \frac{1}{3}$.

Step 1: Regroup 3 by taking 1 from it and writing it as a fraction.

$$3 = 2 + 1 = 2 + \frac{3}{3} = 2\frac{3}{3}$$

Step 2: Rewrite the problem.

$$2\frac{3}{3}$$
$$-\frac{1}{3}$$

Step 3: Subtract the fractions.

$$2\frac{3}{3}$$
$$-\frac{1}{3}$$
$$\frac{2}{3}$$

Step 4: Bring down the whole number.

$$3 - \frac{1}{3} = 2\frac{2}{3}$$

$$2\frac{3}{3}$$
$$-\frac{1}{3}$$
$$2\frac{2}{3}$$

Mixed Fractions

Fido is $18\frac{1}{4}$ inches tall. Moose is $9\frac{3}{4}$ inches tall. How much taller is Fido than Moose?

To solve this problem, subtract.

$$18\frac{1}{4} - 9\frac{3}{4}$$

Step 1: The numerator 3 is greater than the numerator 1, so regroup the whole number 18.

$$18\frac{1}{4} = 17 + \frac{4}{4} + \frac{1}{4} = 17\frac{5}{4}$$
$$-9\frac{3}{4} \qquad\qquad -9\frac{3}{4}$$

Step 2: Subtract the fractions.

$$17\frac{5}{4}$$
$$-9\frac{3}{4}$$
$$\overline{\frac{2}{4}}$$

Step 3: Subtract the whole numbers.

$$17\frac{5}{4}$$
$$-9\frac{3}{4}$$
$$\overline{8\frac{2}{4}}$$

Step 4: Reduce to lowest terms.

$$8\frac{2}{4} = 8\frac{1}{2}$$

Fido is $8\frac{1}{2}$ inches taller than Moose.

Fraction and mixed fraction answers should always be reduced to lowest terms.

Both answers are correct, but an answer in lowest terms is better.

Before you subtract unlike fractions, you need to give them a common denominator.

"I can't find a common denominator!"

If you are stuck, you can find a common denominator by multiplying the two denominators.

A common denominator of $\frac{2}{13}$ and $\frac{1}{4}$ is 13 × 4, or 52.

Multiply the numerator and denominator by the denominator of the other fraction.

$$\frac{2}{13} = \frac{2 \times 4}{13 \times 4} = \frac{8}{52}$$

$$\frac{1}{4} = \frac{1 \times 13}{4 \times 13} = \frac{13}{52}$$

This method may not give you the least common denominator, so be sure to check your final answer to see if it needs to be reduced.

Unlike Fractions

Subtract $\frac{3}{4} - \frac{2}{3}$.

....

Step 1: Find a common denominator.

Multiples of 4 are 4, 8, **12**, 16, . . .
Multiples of 3 are 3, 6, 9, **12**, 15, . . .

The least common multiple of 4 and 3 is 12.
Write both fractions with a denominator of 12.

$$\frac{3}{4} = \frac{3 \times 3}{4 \times 3} = \frac{9}{12} \qquad\qquad \frac{2}{3} = \frac{2 \times 4}{3 \times 4} = \frac{8}{12}$$

Step 2: Write the problem using like fractions.

$$\frac{9}{12} - \frac{8}{12}$$

Step 3: Subtract.

$$\frac{9}{12} - \frac{8}{12} = \frac{9-8}{12} = \frac{1}{12}$$

$$\frac{3}{4} - \frac{2}{3} = \frac{1}{12}$$

Mixed Fractions

Jared has $6\frac{5}{6}$ dozen eggs. He uses $3\frac{1}{2}$ dozen making omelets. How many dozen eggs does Jared have left?

To solve this problem, subtract. $6\frac{5}{6} - 3\frac{1}{2}$

Step 1: Write the problem using like fractions.

$$\frac{1}{2} = \frac{1 \times 3}{1 \times 3} = \frac{3}{6}$$

$$6\frac{5}{6} \qquad 6\frac{5}{6}$$
$$-3\frac{1}{2} \qquad -3\frac{3}{6}$$

Step 2: Subtract the fractions.

$$6\frac{5}{6}$$
$$-3\frac{3}{6}$$
$$\overline{\frac{2}{6}}$$

Step 3: Subtract the whole numbers.

$$6\frac{5}{6}$$
$$-3\frac{3}{6}$$
$$\overline{3\frac{2}{6}}$$

Step 4: Reduce the fraction to lowest terms.

$$\frac{2}{6} = \frac{2 \div 2}{6 \div 2} = \frac{1}{3}$$

$$6\frac{5}{6}$$
$$-3\frac{3}{6}$$
$$\overline{3\frac{2}{6}} = 3\frac{1}{3}$$

Jared has $3\frac{1}{3}$ dozen eggs left.

⑨ Multiplying Fractions

When you multiply fractions, it does not matter if they are like or unlike fractions.

Multiplying Fractions

Multiply $\frac{1}{4} \times \frac{2}{3}$.

This problem can be solved in two ways.

Multiply First:

Step 1: Multiply the numerators.

$$\frac{1}{4} \times \frac{2}{3} = \frac{1 \times 2}{} = \frac{2}{}$$

Step 2: Multiply the denominators.

$$\frac{1}{4} \times \frac{2}{3} = \frac{1 \times 2}{4 \times 3} = \frac{2}{12}$$

Step 3: Reduce the answer to lowest terms.

$$\frac{2}{12} = \frac{2 \div 2}{12 \div 2} = \frac{1}{6}$$

$$\frac{1}{4} \times \frac{2}{3} = \frac{1}{6}$$

Simplify First:

Step 1: Divide the numerator of one fraction and the denominator of the other by a common factor.

Divide 2 and 4 by the common factor 2. Simplify, and write the new number.

$$\frac{1}{\underset{2}{4}} \times \frac{\overset{1}{2}}{3} = \frac{1}{2} \times \frac{1}{3}$$

Step 2: Multiply the numerators.

$$\frac{1}{2} \times \frac{1}{3} = \frac{1 \times 1}{} = \frac{1}{}$$

Step 3: Multiply the denominators.

$$\frac{1}{2} \times \frac{1}{3} = \frac{1 \times 1}{2 \times 3} = \frac{1}{6}$$

$$\frac{1}{4} \times \frac{2}{3} = \frac{1}{6}$$

22

Simplifying

Reducing fractions before you multiply is called simplifying.

Why should you simplify?

Simplifying makes the numbers smaller and easier to multiply.

Simplifying saves you from reducing later.

Whole and Mixed Fractions

A wheelchair relay race is $4\frac{1}{2}$ miles long. Luka will do $\frac{1}{3}$ of the race. How many miles will Luka race?

To solve this problem, multiply.

$$4\frac{1}{2} \times \frac{1}{3}$$

Step 1: Write the whole or mixed numbers as improper fractions. (See page 9.)

$$4\frac{1}{2} = \frac{9}{2}$$

$$4\frac{1}{2} \times \frac{1}{3}$$

$$\frac{9}{2} \times \frac{1}{3}$$

Step 2: Simplify by dividing the 9 and 3 by 3.

$$\frac{\overset{3}{\cancel{9}}}{2} \times \frac{1}{\underset{1}{\cancel{3}}} = \frac{3}{2} \times \frac{1}{1}$$

Step 3: Multiply the numerators. Multiply the denominators.

$$\frac{3}{2} \times \frac{1}{1} = \frac{3 \times 1}{2 \times 1} = \frac{3}{2}$$

Step 4: Write the answer as a mixed fraction.

$$\frac{3}{2} = 1\frac{1}{2}$$

Luka will race $1\frac{1}{2}$ miles.

⑩ Dividing Fractions

Division and multiplication are opposite operations. Divide by a fraction by turning it upside down and then multiplying.

Reciprocals

Reciprocals are two numbers that have a product of 1.

$\frac{1}{5}$ and $\frac{5}{1}$ are reciprocals because $\frac{1 \times 5}{5 \times 1} = \frac{5}{5} = 1$

You can find the reciprocal of a fraction by switching the numerator and denominator.

The reciprocal of $\frac{3}{4}$ is $\frac{4}{3}$.   **The reciprocal of $\frac{1}{2}$ is $\frac{2}{1}$.**

Dividing a Fraction by a Fraction

Divide $\frac{2}{3} \div \frac{1}{2}$.

Step 1: Write the problem using the division sign.

$$\frac{2}{3} \div \frac{1}{2}$$

Step 2: Change the division sign to a multiplication sign. Flip the second fraction upside down to multiply by the reciprocal.

$$\frac{2}{3} \times \frac{2}{1}$$

Step 3: Multiply. $\frac{2}{3} \times \frac{2}{1} = \frac{2 \times 2}{3 \times 1} = \frac{4}{3} = 1\frac{1}{3}$

$$\frac{2}{3} \div \frac{1}{2} = 1\frac{1}{3}$$

ONLY flip the number you are dividing by.

24

Whole and Mixed Fractions

Curtis has a new roll of bubble gum tape. It is 15 inches long. If he tears it into $1\frac{1}{2}$ inch pieces, how many pieces of gum will he have?

To solve this problem, divide.

$$15 \div 1\frac{1}{2}$$

Step 1: Write the problem using the division sign. Change mixed fractions to improper fractions.

$$15 \div 1\frac{1}{2}$$

$$\frac{15}{1} \div \frac{3}{2}$$

Step 2: Change the division sign to a multiplication sign. Flip the second fraction upside down to multiply by the reciprocal.

$$\frac{15}{1} \times \frac{2}{3}$$

Step 3: Simplify.

$$\frac{\overset{5}{\cancel{15}}}{1} \times \frac{2}{\underset{1}{\cancel{3}}}$$

Step 4: Multiply.

$$\frac{5}{1} \times \frac{2}{1} = \frac{5 \times 2}{1 \times 1} = \frac{10}{1} = 10$$

Curtis will have 10 pieces of gum.

Fractions with a 1 in the numerator are easy to divide by. Just multiply by their denominator.

Dividing by $\frac{1}{5}$ is the same as multiplying by 5 because the reciprocal of $\frac{1}{5}$ is $\frac{5}{1}$.

Estimating
With Fractions

(11)

An estimate is an answer that is not exact. A good estimate is an answer that is close to the exact answer.

Fractions

Estimate $\frac{1}{9} + \frac{1}{8} + \frac{3}{8}$.

Estimate by using fractions that work well together.

Step 1: $\frac{1}{9}$ is close to $\frac{1}{8}$. Change $\frac{1}{9}$ to $\frac{1}{8}$.

$$\frac{1}{9} + \frac{1}{8} + \frac{3}{8}$$

$$\frac{1}{8} + \frac{1}{8} + \frac{3}{8}$$

Step 2: Add.

$$\frac{1}{8} + \frac{1}{8} + \frac{3}{8} = \frac{1+1+3}{8} = \frac{5}{8}$$

$\frac{1}{9} + \frac{1}{8} + \frac{3}{8}$ is about $\frac{5}{8}$.

Overestimate and Underestimate

Estimate $\frac{1}{12} + \frac{1}{13}$.

Overestimate: An overestimate is larger than the exact answer. $\frac{1}{12}$ is a little larger than $\frac{1}{13}$. Make $\frac{1}{13}$ a little larger, then add.

$$\frac{1}{12} + \frac{1}{12} = \frac{2}{12} = \frac{1}{6} \qquad \frac{1}{12} + \frac{1}{13} \text{ is about } \frac{1}{6}$$

Underestimate: An underestimate is smaller than the exact answer. $\frac{1}{13}$ is a little smaller than $\frac{1}{12}$. Make $\frac{1}{12}$ a little smaller, then add.

$$\frac{1}{13} + \frac{1}{13} = \frac{2}{13} \qquad \frac{1}{12} + \frac{1}{13} \text{ is about } \frac{2}{13}$$

Both of these answers are good estimates. The exact answer, $\frac{25}{156}$, is between the underestimate, $\frac{2}{13}$, and the overestimate, $\frac{1}{6}$.

Round to a Whole Number

Frank's parents fixed the toilet upstairs, but flooded the living room. Now they need to replace the carpet. The living room is $19\frac{3}{4}$ feet long and $25\frac{1}{3}$ feet wide. About how many square feet of carpet is needed?

To solve this problem, estimate the product of $19\frac{3}{4} \times 25\frac{1}{3}$.

....

Step 1: The problem does not ask for an exact answer. Estimate by finding two whole numbers that are close to the actual numbers.

$19\frac{3}{4}$ **is close to 20.** $\qquad$ $25\frac{1}{3}$ **is close to 25.**

....

Step 2: Multiply the whole numbers. $\qquad$ **20 × 25 = 500**

Frank's parents need about 500 square feet of new carpet.

Why estimate?

Estimate when you don't need an exact answer.

Estimate to make a prediction.

Estimate to see if an exact answer is reasonable.

⑫ Decimals

Decimals are numbers that use a decimal point to separate whole number values from values less than one.

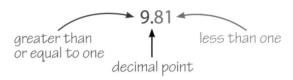

9.81

greater than or equal to one

less than one

decimal point

Decimal Place Value

Decimals follow the same place value pattern as whole numbers. Each place has a value that is ten times the place on its right.

12.34   The digit 1 is in the tens place.
It has a value of 1 ten, or 10.

12.34   The digit 2 is in the ones place.
It has a value of 2 ones, or 2.

12.34   The digit 3 is in the tenths place.
It has a value of 3 tenths, or 0.3.

12.34   The digit 4 is in the hundredths place.
It has a value of 4 hundredths, or 0.04.

You can use **expanded form** to show the place value of each digit. The decimal 12.34 is written in expanded form as:

12.34 = 10 + 2 + 0.3 + 0.04

Reading a Decimal

Luke ran the 100-meter sprint in 14.62 seconds. Read the decimal 14.62.

Step 1: Read the whole number.

14.62
Say "fourteen."

Step 2: Read the decimal point as "and."

14**.**62
Say "and."

Step 3: Read the number after the decimal point as if it were a whole number.

14.**62**
Say "sixty-two."

Step 4: Say the place value name of the last digit.

14.6**2**   **2 is in the hundredths place.**
Say "hundredths."

Read 14.62 as "fourteen and sixty-two hundredths."

Decimal Busters:

Remember: Only say "and" at the decimal point.

All decimal place names end in "ths."

tenth**s**, hundred**ths**, thousand**ths**, ten thousand**ths**. . .

⑬ Equivalent Decimals

Decimals that have the same value, but different names, are called equivalent decimals.

Adding Zeros

This is one whole square.
One of ten equal parts,
or **0.1**, is colored.

Split each of the tenths into
ten equal parts. The same area
is colored, but now there are
10 equal parts out of 100,
or **0.10**, colored.

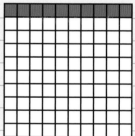

0.1 is the same as 0.10.
You can add zero to the end of the decimal
without changing the value.

You can add any number of zeros
without changing the value of the decimal.

$$0.1 = 0.10 = 0.100 = 0.1000$$

More Zeros

Write two equivalent decimals for 0.3.

Step 1: Add one zero to the right of 0.3.
This is one equivalent decimal.   **0.30**

Step 2: Add another zero to the right of 0.30.   **0.300**

0.3 = 0.30 = 0.300

Whole Numbers

Write the whole number 2 as a decimal.

Step 1: Put a decimal point and a zero   **2.0**
to the right of the whole number.

2 = 2.0

Adding a zero on the right end
of a decimal is really adding nothing.

Think of a decimal in expanded form.

$$0.12 = 0.1 + 0.02$$

Adding a zero to the right is
the same as adding 0.000.

0.000 is nothing.

$$0.12 = 0.120$$

14 Decimals as Fractions

When you hear someone say "seven tenths," are they thinking of the fraction, $\frac{7}{10}$, or the decimal, 0.7?

Writing a Decimal as a Fraction

Write 0.25 as a fraction.

Step 1: The digits to the right of the decimal point are the numerator. Write 25 as the numerator.

$$\frac{25}{\quad}$$

Step 2: The place value of the last digit tells the denominator. The last digit is 5. It is in the hundredths place. Write 100 as the denominator.

$$\frac{25}{100}$$

Step 3: Reduce the fraction to lowest terms. Divide 25 and 100 by their greatest common factor, 25.

$$\frac{25 \div 25}{100 \div 25} = \frac{1}{4}$$

$0.25 = \frac{1}{4}$

> To write a decimal as a fraction, look at the last digit in the decimal.
>
> If it is in the <u>tenths</u> place, the denominator is 10.
> If it is in the <u>hundredths</u> place, the denominator is 100.
> If it is in the <u>thousandths</u> place, the denominator is 1,000.

Writing a Decimal as a Mixed Fraction

Phil drives 10.375 miles to take Melanie home from school. How far is this as a mixed fraction?

Step 1: The decimal 10.375 has digits both left and right of the decimal point. The digits left of the decimal point are the whole number part of a mixed fraction. Write 10 as the whole number.

$$10$$

Step 2: The digits right of the decimal point are the numerator. Write 375 as the numerator.

$$10\frac{375}{}$$

Step 3: The last digit is 5. It is in the thousandths place. Write 1000 as the denominator.

$$10\frac{375}{1000}$$

Step 4: If it is hard to find the greatest common factor, you can reduce more than once. Use any common factor first. Reduce until the fraction is in lowest terms. Divide 375 and 1,000 by 5 first. Reduce again by dividing 75 and 200 by 25.

$$\frac{375 \div 5}{1000 \div 5} = \frac{75}{200}$$

$$\frac{75 \div 25}{200 \div 25} = \frac{3}{8}$$

$$10\frac{375}{1000} = 10\frac{3}{8}$$

Phil drives $10\frac{3}{8}$ miles to take Melanie home from school.

⑮ Fractions as Decimals

Fractions with denominators that are powers of ten are easy to write as decimals.

Powers of Ten

Write $\frac{3}{100}$ as a decimal.

Step 1: There is no whole number part, so write a zero to the left of the decimal point.   **0.**

Step 2: The denominator is 100, so the decimal ends in the hundredths place.   **0.__ __**

Step 3: Write the numerator, 3, in the hundredths place.   **0.__3**

Step 4: Use zeros as place holders to keep the 3 in the right place.   **0.03**

$\frac{3}{100} = 0.03$

Write $1\frac{1}{2}$ as a decimal.

Step 1: Look at the fraction part. The denominator, 2, is not a power of ten. Write an equivalent fraction with a denominator that is a power of ten.

Powers of ten are the products when 10 is multiplied by itself.
$10 \times 10 = 100$;
$10 \times 10 \times 10 = 1,000$;
$10 \times 10 \times 10 \times 10 = 10,000$;
etc.

$2 \times 5 = 10$, so multiply the numerator and denominator by 5.

$\frac{1}{2} = \frac{1 \times 5}{2 \times 5} = \frac{5}{10}$

Step 2: The whole number part is 1, so write 1, then the decimal point.   **1.**

34

Step 3: The denominator is 10, so the decimal ends in the tenths place.

1._

Step 4: Write the numerator, 5, in the tenths place.

$1\frac{1}{2} = 1.5$

1.5

Division

Write $\frac{1}{8}$ as a decimal.

> Fractions are a way to show division.
>
> The fraction bar can be read as "divided by."

Step 1: You can write a fraction as a decimal by dividing the numerator by the denominator. $\frac{1}{8}$ means 1 ÷ 8. Write this using the long division symbol.

$$8\overline{)1}$$

Step 2: Write the number you are dividing as a decimal. Start with one zero. Place another decimal point in the answer directly above the decimal point.

$$8\overline{)1.0}$$

Step 3: Divide the same way you divide whole numbers. Add zeros to the end of the number you are dividing until you have no remainder.

$\frac{1}{8} = 0.125$

```
      0.125
   8)1.000
    - 8
      20
    - 16
      40
    - 40
       0
```

⑯ **Comparing** Decimals

Decimals are compared using place value.

Comparing Decimals

In January, stock for the OrangeFunk Company had a value of $12.59 a share. In June, the same stock had a value of $12.82. During which month was the value higher?

To solve this problem, compare $12.59 and $12.82.

Step 1: Money values are often written as decimals. To compare decimals, line up the decimal points.

↓
$12.59
$12.82

Step 2: Start at the left digit on each number. Compare digits that have the same place value. Both numbers have a 1 in the tens place. Both numbers have a 2 in the ones place. In the tenths place, 5 is less than 8, so $12.59 is less than $12.82.

$12.59
$12.82
↑

$12.59 < $12.82

The problem asks which month had a higher value. The higher value is $12.82, which was for the month of June.

The OrangeFunk Company had a higher value in June than it did in January.

Compare 0.23 and 0.217.

Step 1: Line up the decimal points.

0.23
0.217

Step 2: Add zeros to the right to give each number the same number of digits.

0.230
0.217

Step 3: Compare the digits from left to right. Both numbers have a 0 in the ones place. Both numbers have a 2 in the tenths place. In the hundredths place, 3 is greater than 1, so 0.23 is greater than 0.217.

0.2**3**0
0.2**1**7

0.23 > 0.217

> For whole numbers, the number with the most digits is always the greatest.
> This is NOT true for decimals. 0.23 has fewer digits, but a greater value, than 0.217.

Order 0.12, 0.224, and 0.21 from least to greatest.

Step 1: Line up the decimal points.

0.12
0.224
0.21

Step 2: Add zeros to the right to give each number the same number of digits.

0.120
0.224
0.210

Step 3: Compare the digits from left to right. All three numbers have 0 in the ones place. In the tenths place, 1 is less than 2. So, 0.120 is the least, or smallest number. Cross it off.

~~0.120~~
0.**2**24
0.**2**10

Step 4: Compare the remaining numbers, starting in the next place. In the hundredths place, 1 is less than 2. The next smallest number is 0.210.

~~0.120~~
0.2**2**4
0.2**1**0

Write the decimals from smallest to largest. Use the original decimals, not the ones to which you added zeros.

0.12, 0.21, 0.224

⑰ Rounding Decimals

Rounding gives you a rough idea
of a value. Rounding decimals is done in
the same way as rounding whole numbers.

Rounding to Whole Numbers

Charles can hold his breath underwater for 42.37 seconds.
Round 42.37 to the nearest whole second.

Step 1: The nearest whole
second means the ones place.
Find the ones place.

> **4_2_.37**

Step 2: Look at the digit
one place to its right.
The tenths place is one
place right of the ones place.

> **42._3_7**

If the digit is 5 or greater, round up
      to the next whole number.
If the digit is less than 5, round down. When you round down,
      the digit in the place you are rounding to stays the same.

3 is less than 5, so round down.
Leave the 2 in the ones place. Drop
the digits after the decimal point.   **42.37 rounds down to 42.**

Rounding to Decimal Places

One gallon of water weighs 8.32797 pounds. Round the weight of water to the nearest hundredth of a pound.

Step 1: Find the hundredths place.   8.3<u>2</u>797

Step 2: Look at the digit   8.32<u>7</u>97
one place to its right.
The thousandths place is one
place right of the hundredths place.

7 is 5 or greater, so round up.
Change the 2 in the hundredths
place to 3. Drop the digits after
the hundredths place.   **8.32797 rounds to 8.33.**

To the nearest hundredth of a pound, one gallon of water weighs 8.33 pounds.

Whole Numbers vs. Decimals

There is only one difference between rounding whole numbers and rounding decimals.

When you round whole numbers, you write zeros to the right of the place you are rounding to.

433 rounded to the hundreds place is **4<u>00</u>**.

When you round decimals, you drop the digits to the right of the place you are rounding to.

0.52 rounded to the tenths place is **0.5.**

⑱ Adding Decimals

When you add any numbers, you can only add digits that have the same place value.

Adding Decimals

Add 0.521 + 0.37.

Step 1: Write the numbers in a column. Line up decimal points. When the decimal points are lined up, all of the places are also lined up.

$$\begin{array}{r} 0.521 \\ + 0.37 \\ \hline \end{array}$$

Step 2: One of the numbers ends in the hundredths place. The other ends in the thousandths. To make it easier to add, you can add zeros to the right to give each number the same number of digits.

$$\begin{array}{r} 0.521 \\ + 0.370 \\ \hline \end{array}$$

Step 3: Add each place, beginning on the right. Add the thousandths.

$$\begin{array}{r} 0.521 \\ + 0.370 \\ \hline 1 \end{array}$$

Step 4: Add the hundredths.

$$\begin{array}{r} 0.521 \\ + 0.370 \\ \hline 91 \end{array}$$

Step 5: Add the tenths. Write the decimal point in the answer.

$$\begin{array}{r} 0.521 \\ + 0.370 \\ \hline .891 \end{array}$$

Step 6: Add the ones.

$$\begin{array}{r} 0.521 \\ + 0.370 \\ \hline .891 \end{array}$$

0.521 + 0.37 = 0.891

Adding Whole Numbers and Decimals

Ellis says that 65.21 + 3 = 65.51. Is he correct?

To solve this problem, add 65.21 and 3, then check the answer.

Step 1: Write the numbers in a column.
3 is a whole number. The decimal point
in a whole number is right of the ones place.

$$\begin{array}{r} 65.21 \\ +\ \ 3 \\ \hline \end{array}$$

Step 2: Add zeros to give each number the
same number of digits.

$$\begin{array}{r} 65.21 \\ +\ 3.00 \\ \hline \end{array}$$

Step 3: Add the hundredths.

$$\begin{array}{r} 65.21 \\ +\ 3.00 \\ \hline 1 \end{array}$$

Step 4: Add the tenths.
Write the decimal point in the answer.

$$\begin{array}{r} 65.21 \\ +\ 3.00 \\ \hline .21 \end{array}$$

Step 5: Add the ones.

$$\begin{array}{r} 65.21 \\ +\ 3.00 \\ \hline 8.21 \end{array}$$

Step 6: Add the tens.

$$\begin{array}{r} 65.21 \\ +\ 3.00 \\ \hline 68.21 \end{array}$$

Step 7: Compare the sum
with the sum Ellis found.

65.21 + 3 = 68.21
Ellis says 65.21 + 3 = 65.51

Ellis is not correct.

⑲ Regrouping to Add

When you add, you can regroup decimals and carry them to the next place value.

Regrouping

Regrouping names values in a different way.

10 ones can be regrouped as **1 ten**.
10 tenths can be regrouped as **1 one**.
10 hundredths can be regrouped as **1 tenth**.

Adding Decimals

Add 6.27 + 1.92.

Step 1: Write the numbers in a column.
Line up the decimal points.

$$\begin{array}{r} 6.27 \\ + 1.92 \\ \hline \end{array}$$

Step 2: Add the hundredths.

$$\begin{array}{r} 6.27 \\ + 1.92 \\ \hline 9 \end{array}$$

Step 3: Add the tenths. 9 + 2 = 11.
Regroup 11 tenths as 1 one and 1 tenth.
Carry the regrouped one to the ones place.
Write the decimal point in your answer.

$$\begin{array}{r} 1 \\ 6.27 \\ + 1.92 \\ \hline .19 \end{array}$$

Step 4: Add the ones. Remember to add the regrouped 1.

6.27 + 1.92 = 8.19

$$\begin{array}{r} 1 \\ 6.27 \\ + 1.92 \\ \hline 8.19 \end{array}$$

Adding Multiple Decimals

The table shows how much Alisha's tomato plant grew each week. How many inches did it grow in four weeks?

WEEK	INCHES
1	2.1
2	5
3	6.23
4	4.7

Step 1: Write the numbers from each of the four weeks in a column. Line up the decimal points.

```
  2.1
  5
  6.23
+ 4.7
```

Step 2: Add zeros to give each number the same number of digits.

```
  2.10
  5.00
  6.23
+ 4.70
```

Step 3: Add the hundredths.
0 + 0 + 3 + 0 = 3

```
  2.10
  5.00
  6.23
+ 4.70
     3
```

Step 4: Add the tenths.
1 + 0 + 2 + 7 = 10
Regroup 10 tenths as 1 one.
Write the decimal point
in your answer.

```
  2.10
  5.00
  6.23
+ 4.70
   .03
```

Step 5: Add the ones.
1 + 2 + 5 + 6 + 4 = 18

```
  2.10
  5.00
  6.23
+ 4.70
 18.03
```

Alisha's tomato plant grew 18.03 inches in 4 weeks.

⑳ Subtracting Decimals

When you know how to subtract whole numbers, you also know how to subtract decimals. The only difference is the decimal point.

Subtracting Money

Subtract $19.82 – $12.71.

Step 1: Write the numbers in a column. Line up the decimal points.

$19.82
– $12.71

Step 2: Subtract as you would whole numbers. Begin on the right. Subtract one place value at a time. Subtract the hundredths.

$19.82
– $12.71
1

Step 3: Subtract the tenths. Write the decimal point in the answer.

$19.82
– $12.71
.11

Step 4: Subtract the ones.

$19.82
– $12.71
7.11

Step 5: Subtract the tens. This is a money value, so write the dollar sign in the answer.

$19.82
– $12.71
$ 7.11

$19.82 – $12.71 = $7.11

Money values are written using decimals.

With money values, write a decimal point and the dollar sign in the answer.

44

Decimal Terms

decimal numbers—Numbers that are decimals. We usually just call them decimals.

decimal fractions—Decimals that have a value less than one. Some decimal fractions are 0.6, 0.471, and 0.84.

mixed decimals—Decimals that have a value greater than one. Some mixed decimals are 1.01, 25.6, and 6.178. Mixed decimals have a whole number part and a decimal fraction part.

Subtracting Decimals

Subtract 0.52 from 2.863.

Step 1: This problem uses the words *subtract* and *from*. It means to start with the second number, and take the first number from it.
Write the numbers in a column.
Line up the decimal points.

$$\begin{array}{r} 2.863 \\ -\ 0.52 \\ \hline \end{array}$$

Step 2: Add zeros to give each number the same number of digits.

$$\begin{array}{r} 2.863 \\ -\ 0.520 \\ \hline \end{array}$$

Step 3: Subtract the thousandths.

$$\begin{array}{r} 2.863 \\ -\ 0.520 \\ \hline 3 \end{array}$$

Step 4: Subtract the hundredths.

$$\begin{array}{r} 2.863 \\ -\ 0.520 \\ \hline 43 \end{array}$$

Step 5: Subtract the tenths.
Write the decimal point in the answer.

$$\begin{array}{r} 2.863 \\ -\ 0.520 \\ \hline .343 \end{array}$$

Step 6: Subtract the ones.

2.863 − 0.52 = 2.343

$$\begin{array}{r} 2.863 \\ -\ 0.520 \\ \hline 2.343 \end{array}$$

Regrouping to Subtract

When subtracting, you regroup by "borrowing" from the next larger place value.

Subtracting Decimals

Louie's computer has 2 hard drives. One has 9.5 GB of space left. The other has 7.8 GB left. How much more space does the first drive have left?

To solve this problem, subtract.	**9.5 – 7.8**

Step 1: Write the numbers in a column. Line up decimal points.

$$\begin{array}{r} 9.5 \\ -\ 7.8 \end{array}$$

Step 2: Look in the tenths column. You can not subtract 8 from 5. You can regroup 9 ones and 5 tenths as 8 ones and 15 tenths.

Write the regrouped values above each column. Cross out the original digits to remind yourself that they have been regrouped.

$$\begin{array}{r} {}^{8}\!\!\!\not{9}.{}^{15}\!\!\!\not{5} \\ -\ 7.8 \end{array}$$

Step 3: Subtract the tenths. Write the decimal point in the answer.

$$\begin{array}{r} {}^{8}\!\!\!\not{9}.{}^{15}\!\!\!\not{5} \\ -\ 7.8 \\ \hline .7 \end{array}$$

Step 4: Subtract the ones.

There are 1.7 GB more space left in the first drive.

$$\begin{array}{r} {}^{8}\!\!\!\not{9}.{}^{15}\!\!\!\not{5} \\ -\ 7.8 \\ \hline 1.7 \end{array}$$

Decimal Subtraction

When you subtract decimals:

- Line up the decimal points.
- Write zeros on the right to give decimals the same number of digits.
- Subtract from right to left.
- Regroup whenever you need to. Regrouping decimals is the same as regrouping whole numbers.

Subtracting Across Zeros

Krista is buying a 120-GB hard drive for $63.44. She has $100. How much will she have left after her purchase?

To solve this problem, subtract. $100 − $63.44

Step 1: Write the numbers in a column.
Line up decimal points. Add zeros to
give each number the same number of digits.

$$\begin{array}{r} \$100.00 \\ -\ \$\ \ 63.44 \\ \hline \end{array}$$

Step 2: You must regroup before you
can subtract. There are no tenths, ones,
or tens to regroup.
Regroup 1 hundred as 10 tens.
Regroup 1 ten as 10 ones.
Regroup 1 one as 10 tenths.
Regroup 1 tenth as 10 hundredths.

$$\begin{array}{r} 9\ 9\ 9 \\ \cancel{10}\cancel{10}\ \cancel{10}\cancel{10} \\ \$100.00 \\ -\ \$\ \ 63.44 \\ \hline \end{array}$$

Step 3: Subtract in each place, from right to left.
Remember to write the decimal point and
dollar sign in the answer.

$$\begin{array}{r} 9\ 9\ 9 \\ \cancel{10}\cancel{10}\ \cancel{10}\cancel{10} \\ \$100.00 \\ -\ \$\ \ 63.44 \\ \hline \$\ \ 36.56 \end{array}$$

Krista will have $36.56 left.

㉒ Multiplying Decimals

When you multiply decimals,
you do not need to line up the
decimal points.

Multiplying Whole Numbers and Decimals

A city bus pass costs Rob $3.75 each week. How much does it cost him to ride the bus for 5 weeks?

To solve this problem, multiply.	$3.75 × 5

Step 1: Write the numbers in a column.
You do not need to line up the decimal points.

$$\begin{array}{r} \$3.75 \\ \times \quad 5 \\ \hline \end{array}$$

Step 2: Ignore the decimal points.
Multiply the factors as whole numbers.
Multiply one place value at a time, regrouping
when needed.

$$\begin{array}{r} {\scriptstyle 3\ 2} \\ \$3.75 \\ \times \quad 5 \\ \hline 1875 \end{array}$$

Step 3: Count the total number of places after the decimal point in both factors.

$3.75 has 2 decimal places.
5 has 0 decimal places.
There are 2 total decimal places.

Step 4: The total number of decimal places
in the factors tells the total number of decimal
places in the answer. Count 2 decimal places from
the right. Place the decimal point in the answer.

$$\begin{array}{r} {\scriptstyle 3\ 2} \\ \$3.75 \\ \times \quad 5 \\ \hline \$18.75 \\ {\scriptstyle 2\ 1} \end{array}$$

**It costs Rob $18.75 to
ride the bus for 5 weeks.**

48

Multiplication Terms

factors—The numbers being multiplied.

product—The answer to a multiplication problem.

Multiplying Decimals

Multiply 8.6 by 0.003.

Step 1: Write the numbers in a column.
You do not need to line up the decimal points.

$$\begin{array}{r} 8.6 \\ \times\ 0.003 \end{array}$$

Step 2: Ignore the decimal points.
Multiply the factors as whole numbers.
Treat 0.003 as the whole number 3.

$$\begin{array}{r} 8.6 \\ \times\ 0.003 \\ \hline 258 \end{array}$$

Step 3: Count the total number of places after the decimal points in both factors.

8.6 has 1 decimal place.
0.003 has 3 decimal places.
There are 4 total decimal places.

Step 4: Count 4 decimal places from the right. Since there are only 3 digits in the product, add a zero to the left to place the decimal point. Write a zero in the ones place as a place holder.

8.6 × 0.003 = 0.0258

$$\begin{array}{r} 8.6 \\ \times\ 0.003 \\ \hline 0.0258 \end{array}$$

4 3 2 1

Problem Buster:
Solve money
problems by knowing
how to use decimals!

㉓ Dividing Decimals

When dividing decimals, put the decimal point in the answer before you divide.

Division Terms

quotient—The answer to a division problem. $6 \div 2 = \mathbf{3}$

dividend—The number you are dividing. $\mathbf{6} \div 2 = 3$

divisor—The number you are dividing by. $6 \div \mathbf{2} = 3$

Dividing Decimals by Whole Numbers

At a steady pace, it took Faith 2 hours to hike a trail that is 1.9 miles long. How far did she hike each hour?

To solve this problem, divide.	$1.9 \div 2$
Step 1: Write this problem using the long division symbol.	$2\overline{)1.9}$
Step 2: Place the decimal point in the answer directly above the decimal point in the dividend.	$2\overline{)1.9}$ with decimal point above
Step 3: Divide the same way you divide whole numbers. Can you take any 2s from 1? No. Write a zero above the ones place as a placeholder. Can you take any 2s from 19? Yes. You can take 9. Write a 9 in the tenths place. Multiply. $2 \times 9 = 18$. Subtract. $19 - 18 = 1$.	$\begin{array}{r} 0.9 \\ 2\overline{)1.9} \\ -1.8 \\ \hline 1 \end{array}$

Step 4: You have a remainder of 1. Add a zero to the number you are dividing. Bring down the zero. Can you take any 2s from 10? Yes. You can take 5. Write a 5 in the hundredths place. Multiply. $2 \times 5 = 10$. Subtract. $10 - 10 = 0$. There is no remainder. You are done. **$1.9 \div 2 = 0.95$.** **Faith hiked 0.95 miles each hour.**

```
    0.95
2)1.90
  -18
   10
  -10
    0
```

Dividing Whole Numbers

It took Faith 4 hours to hike a trail that was 3 miles long. How far did she hike each hour?

Step 1: Write this problem using the long division symbol.

```
4)3
```

Step 2: Write the number you are dividing as a decimal. Start with one zero. Place a decimal point in the answer directly above the decimal point.

```
     .
4)3.0
```

Step 3: Divide the same way you divide whole numbers. Add another zero on the right. Add zeros and divide until there is no remainder.

$3 \div 4 = 0.75$.
Faith hiked 0.75 miles each hour.

```
    0.75
2)3.00
  -28
   20
  -20
    0
```

The long division symbol makes it easy to place the decimal point in the answer.

㉔ Dividing by a Decimal

You can move the decimal point in division, as long as you move it in both numbers.

Dividing a Whole Number by a Decimal

Becki's cat went to the vet and got some medicine. The medicine bottle holds 4 ounces of medicine. The cat needs 0.25 ounces of medicine each day. How many days will the bottle last?

To solve this problem, divide. $4 \div 0.25$

Step 1: Write the problem using long division. Make the divisor (0.25) a whole number by moving the decimal point two places right. Move the same number of places in the dividend. Add zeros to fill in places on the right.

$$0.25\overline{)4}$$

$$25\overline{)400}$$

Step 2: Divide.

$$
\begin{array}{r}
16 \\
25\overline{)400} \\
-25 \\
\hline
150 \\
-150 \\
\hline
0
\end{array}
$$

$4 \div 0.25 = 16$
The bottle will last 16 days.

Dividing a Decimal by a Decimal

Divide 2.6 ÷ 0.5.

Step 1: Write the problem using long division. Make the divisor (0.5) a whole number by moving the decimal point one place right. Move the same number of places in the dividend.

$$0.5\overline{)2.6}$$
$$5\overline{)26}$$

Step 2: Divide. There is a remainder, 1. Do not write a remainder.

$$\begin{array}{r} 5 \\ 5\overline{)26} \\ -25 \\ \hline 1 \end{array}$$

Step 3: Add a decimal point and a zero to the dividend. Write a decimal point in the answer. Continue to divide, adding zeros to the dividend until there is no remainder.

$$\begin{array}{r} 5.2 \\ 5\overline{)26.0} \\ -25 \\ \hline 10 \\ -10 \\ \hline 0 \end{array}$$

2.6 ÷ 0.5 = 5.2

Decimal Division

1. **Make the divisor a whole number.** Move the decimal point the same number of places in the divisor and dividend.

2. **Place the decimal point in the answer.** Put the decimal point in the answer directly above the decimal point in the dividend.

3. **Divide.** Divide as you would divide a whole number. Add zeros to the right of the dividend until there is no remainder.

㉕ Terminating and Repeating

Sometimes when you divide you add zeros on the right, but the remainder is never zero.

Kinds of Decimals

A **terminating decimal** ends.

A **repeating decimal** has a pattern that happens over and over without end.

Terminating Decimals

Write $\frac{5}{8}$ as a decimal.

Step 1: Divide the numerator by the denominator. Write the problem using the long division symbol.
Add a decimal point and at least one zero.

$$8\overline{)5.0}$$

Step 2: Divide. Add zeros to the end of the number you are dividing until you have a zero remainder.

0.625 is a terminating decimal. It ends with a 5 in the thousandths place.

$$\frac{5}{8} = 0.625$$

$$
\begin{array}{r}
0.625 \\
8\overline{)5.000} \\
-48 \\
\hline
20 \\
-16 \\
\hline
40 \\
-40 \\
\hline
0
\end{array}
$$

Repeating Decimals

Write $\frac{2}{3}$ as a decimal.

Step 1: Divide the numerator by the denominator. Use the long division symbol. Add a decimal point and at least one zero.

$$3\overline{)2.0}$$

Step 2: Divide. When you subtract 18 from 20, the remainder is 2. Add another zero. Now you have another 20.

$$\begin{array}{r} 0.6 \\ 3\overline{)2.00} \\ -18 \\ \hline 20 \end{array}$$

Step 3: Divide again. When you subtract 18 from 20, the remainder is 2 again. The same remainder, 2, will repeat forever.

$$\begin{array}{r} 0.66\ldots \\ 3\overline{)2.00} \\ -18 \\ \hline 20 \\ -18 \\ \hline 2 \end{array}$$

Step 4: 0.66 . . . is a repeating decimal. Repeating decimals are written using a bar over the digits that repeat. Draw a bar over the 6.

$$0.66\ldots$$

$$0.\overline{6}$$

$$\frac{2}{3} = 0.\overline{6}$$

Repeating Decimals as Fractions

Write $0.\overline{54}$ as a fraction.

Step 1: Write the repeating digits as the numerator.

$$\underline{54}$$

Step 2: Count the number of repeating digits. There are 2 digits that repeat.

$$\frac{12}{54}$$

Step 3: Write the same number of 9s in the denominator as there are repeating digits. There are 2, so the denominator is 99.

$$\frac{54}{99}$$

Step 4: Reduce to lowest terms.

$$0.\overline{54} = \frac{6}{11}$$

$$\frac{54}{99} = \frac{54 \div 9}{99 \div 9} = \frac{6}{11}$$

㉖ Powers of Ten

You can multiply or divide by a power of ten by moving the decimal point.

Powers of Ten

Powers of ten are 10 and products of 10 multiplied by itself.

10 × 10 = 100, so 100 is a power of 10.
10 × 10 × 10 = 1,000, so 1,000 is a power of 10.

Powers of ten have a one, followed by zeros.
10, 100, 1,000, 10,000, 100,000, . . .

Multiplication Patterns

Multiply 1.25 × 10 and 1.25 × 100. Do you see a pattern?

Step 1: Multiply 10 × 1.25.

1.25 × 10 = 12.5

$$\begin{array}{r} 1.25 \\ \times\ 10 \\ \hline 12.50 \end{array}$$

Step 2: Multiply 100 × 1.25.

1.25 × 100 = 125

$$\begin{array}{r} 1.25 \\ \times 100 \\ \hline 125.0 \end{array}$$

Step 3: What pattern do you see?

1.25 × 10 = 12.5
1.25 × 100 = 125

The digits stay the same, but the decimal point moves. It moves one place to the right for each zero in the power of 10.

Mental Multiplication

Multiply 0.68 by 1,000 mentally.

Step 1: Move the decimal point one place *right* for each zero in the power of ten.

$0.68 \times 1,000$

0.68

1 2 3

680

There are three zeros in 1,000, so move the decimal point three places *right*.

$0.68 \times 1,000 = 680$

Mental Division

Divide 73.5 by 10 mentally.

Step 1: Division by a power of ten moves the decimal point *left* one place for each zero.
There is one zero in 10, so move the decimal point one place left.

$73.5 \div 10$

73.5

1

7.35

$73.5 \div 10 = 7.35$

Divide 73.5 by 100 mentally.

Step 1: Division by a power of ten moves the decimal point left one place for each zero.
There are two zeros in 100, so move the decimal point two places left.

$73.5 \div 100$

73.5

2 1

0.735

$73.5 \div 100 = 0.735$

Multiplication by
a power of ten moves
the decimal point to the **right**.

Division by a power
of ten moves the decimal
point to the **left**.

㉗ Percents

Percent means per hundred.
Percents are the same as fractions
with a denominator of 100.

Percents

Percents are written using the percent sign, %.

50% is read as "50 percent."
50% means 50 per 100, or $\frac{50}{100}$.

Writing a Decimal as a Percent

Write 0.65 as a percent.

Step 1: Move the decimal point two places
to the right.

0.65

1 2
65

Step 2: Write the percent sign.

65%

0.65 = 65%

100% is $\frac{100}{100}$, or 1.
You can multiply any number
by 1 without changing its value.

When you change a decimal to a
percent, you are multiplying it by 100%.
Multiplying by 100 moves the decimal
point two places to the right.
Then add the percent sign.

Writing a Fraction as a Percent

The music store at the mall is taking $\frac{1}{2}$ off the price of all posters. What percent are they taking off the price of posters?

To solve this problem, write $\frac{1}{2}$ as a percent.

....

Step 1: Write the fraction as a decimal. Divide the numerator (2) by the denominator (1).

$$
\begin{array}{r}
0.5 \\
2\overline{)1.0} \\
-1\,0 \\
\hline
0
\end{array}
$$

....

Step 2: Write the decimal (0.5) as a percent. Move the decimal point two places right. Add the percent sign.

0.50 = 50%

1 2

They are taking 50% off the price of all posters.

Common Fractions

Some fractions are used often enough that you should memorize their decimal and percent equivalents.

fraction	decimal	percent
$\frac{1}{4}$	0.25	25%
$\frac{1}{2}$	0.5	50%
$\frac{3}{4}$	0.75	75%
$\frac{1}{3}$	$0.\overline{33}$	$33\frac{1}{3}\%$

㉘ Estimating With Decimals

You can use estimation to find
a fast, but not exact, answer.

Rounding to a Place Value

*Justin has $110. He is buying an
amplifier for $91.75. He also needs
new guitar strings that cost $15.88.
Does he have enough money for
both items?*

To solve this problem, estimate
the sum of $91.75 and $15.88.

Step 1: Round each number before
you add. If the addends have the
same number of digits, round to the
greatest place value. If the addends
have a different number of digits,
round to the greatest place value of
the smaller number.

$91.75 rounds to $92
$15.88 rounds to $16

Step 2: Add the rounded numbers.

$92
+ $16
$108

Estimate–
An answer that
is not exact;
a reasonable guess.

Step 3: Compare your estimate
with how much money Justin has.

**Justin has $110. The estimate total is $108.
Justin has enough money for both items.**

Rounding to the Greatest Place Value

Estimate 6.102 × 0.52.
One Way:

Step 1: You can estimate by rounding each number to its greatest place value.

The greatest place value of 6.102 is the ones place.

6.102 rounds to 6.

The greatest place value of 0.52 is the tenths place.

0.52 rounds to 0.5.

> *Greatest Place Value–*
> *The first place from*
> *the left in a number that*
> *has a digit other than zero.*
>
> *0.05 - the greatest place*
> *value is the*
> *hundredths place.*

Step 2: Multiply the rounded numbers.

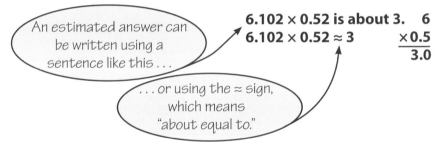

An estimated answer can be written using a sentence like this . . .

. . . or using the ≈ sign, which means "about equal to."

6.102 × 0.52 is about 3.
6.102 × 0.52 ≈ 3

$$\begin{array}{r} 6 \\ \times\,0.5 \\ \hline 3.0 \end{array}$$

Another Way:

Step 1: You can estimate by rounding each number to the greatest place value of the smaller number.

The smaller number is 0.52. The greatest place value of 0.52 is the tenths place. Round each number to the tenths place.

6.102 rounds to 6.1.
0.52 rounds to 0.5.

Step 2: Multiply the rounded numbers.

6.102 × 0.52 ≈ 3.05

$$\begin{array}{r} 6.1 \\ \times\,0.5 \\ \hline 3.05 \end{array}$$

Further Reading

Books

Cummings, Alyece B., M.A. *Painless Fractions*. Hauppauge, New York: Barron's Educational Series Inc., 2012.

McKellar, Danica. *Math Doesn't Suck: How to Survive Middle School Math Without Losing your Mind or Breaking a Nail*. New York: Penguin Group, 2008.

Shields, Charles. *How to Work with Fractions, Decimals & Percents, Grades 5–8*. Westminster, Calif.: Teacher Created Resources, Inc., 2011.

Zev, Marc, Kevin B. Segal, and Nathan Levy. *101 Things Everyone Should Know About Math*. Washington, D.C.: Science, Naturally!, 2010.

Internet Addresses

Banfill, J. AAA Math "Fractions." © 2012.
<http://www.aaamath.com/fra.htm>

———. AAA Math "Decimals." © 2012.
<http://www.aaamath.com/dec.htm>

The Math Forum. "Ask Dr. Math." © 1994–2012.
<http://mathforum.org/library/drmath/sets/elem_fractions.html>

Index